PRESIDENT
Theodore
Roosevelt

TAMARA ORR STAATS

Boston, Massachusetts
Chandler, Arizona
Glenview, Illinois
Upper Saddle River, New Jersey

Illustrations

Opener, 1, 2, 3, 4, 8, 10, 11, 15 Dan Bridy; 13 Joe LeMonnier.

Photographs

Every effort has been made to secure permission and provide appropriate credit for photographic material.
The publisher deeply regrets any omission and pledges to correct errors called to its attention in subsequent editions.

Unless otherwise acknowledged, all photographs are the property of Pearson Education, Inc.

Photo locators denoted as follows: Top (T), Center (C), Bottom (B), Left (L), Right (R), Background (Bkgd)

5 Prints & Photographs Division, LC-USZ62-113665/Library of Congress; 6 Prints & Photographs Division, LC-USZ62-11990/
Library of Congress; 7 Prints & Photographs Division, LC-DIG-pga-01946/Library of Congress; 9 Stereograph Cards
Collection, Prints & Photographs Division, LC-DIG-stereo-1s02050/Library of Congress; 12 Prints & Photographs Division,
LC-USZC4-11867/Library of Congress; 14 Medioimages/Photodisc/Thinkstock.

ISBN-13: 978-0-328-67626-2
ISBN-10: 0-328-67626-8

3 4 5 6 7 8 9 10 V0FL 15 14 13 12

A President Who Loved Nature

Do you enjoy nature? Do you like hiking up high mountains or through shady forests? If so, you are a lot like one of our country's great presidents, Theodore "Teddy" Roosevelt. He worked hard to protect America's **wilderness** areas.

Early Years

Theodore Roosevelt was born in New York City in 1858. He was a sickly child. His father believed exercise would make his son stronger. He built a gym so Theodore could exercise. It worked! Roosevelt enjoyed being active his entire life.

Once, on a hunting trip, Roosevelt refused to shoot an old bear. Then a newspaper published this cartoon. Soon, stores were selling stuffed animals they called "teddy bears."

As a child, Roosevelt loved to study nature. He began to collect things he found, such as snake skins and animal skulls. As an adult, Roosevelt became a hunter. Sometimes, he came home from hunting with additions to his collection.

College and Marriage

Roosevelt became interested in government at Harvard University. There, a friend introduced him to Alice Lee. Four years after their marriage, Alice died. It was just days after she gave birth to their child. Roosevelt's mother also died on the same day.

Later, Roosevelt married Edith Carow and they raised six children.

Roosevelt out West

The deaths made Roosevelt sad. He decided to move west, hoping that would cheer him up. For two years, Roosevelt lived the life of a cowboy and rancher. In this beautiful part of the country, his love of wildlife and nature grew even stronger.

Several years later, Roosevelt married Edith Carow. Together, they raised six children.

The Rough Riders

In 1898, the United States declared war on Spain. Roosevelt was eager to fight. He organized a group of cowboys and ranchers called the Rough Riders. They won a big battle in Cuba, an island country south of Florida.

Roosevelt and the Rough Riders in Cuba

Governor and Vice President

Roosevelt came home a hero. He was asked to run for governor of New York State and won the election in 1898.

As governor, Roosevelt made sure workers were treated fairly. Roosevelt had new ideas. Government leaders began to notice him.

In 1900, President William McKinley turned to Roosevelt. He asked Roosevelt to run for election as his vice president. Roosevelt drew huge crowds everywhere they went. They won the election.

A McKinley-Roosevelt campaign poster

President

On September 6, 1901, something terrible happened. President McKinley was shot after giving a speech. He died a week later. Suddenly, Roosevelt was president. He was 42 years old. That made him the country's youngest president ever.

A Square Deal

As president, Roosevelt promised Americans a "Square Deal." He wanted businesses to be fair to workers.

In 1902, coal miners went on **strike**. They wanted better pay and shorter work days. Roosevelt talked with the miners and the coal mine owners. He was able to help them come to an agreement. The workers returned to their jobs.

Speak Softly

President Roosevelt wanted the country to be a world leader. He said that leaders must "speak softly and carry a big stick." He meant that the United States should first try to solve problems by talking with other countries. But if talking failed, the country should be willing to use force. Roosevelt worked to strengthen the army and navy.

Panama Canal

For years, people had dreamed about a shortcut that ships could take between the Atlantic and Pacific oceans. President Roosevelt helped make this happen. For 10 years, 30,000 men worked to build the Panama **Canal**. When it was completed in 1914, it saved ships thousands of miles of travel.

Routes Before and After the Panama Canal

San Francisco

NORTH AMERICA

New York

Atlantic Ocean

Pacific Ocean

Panama Canal

Equator

SOUTH AMERICA

— Shipping route before building of canal

— Shipping route after building of canal

Cape Horn

ANTARCTICA

Saving the Wilderness

Roosevelt was a strong supporter of **conservation**. He wanted to protect the wildlife and lands he loved. As president, Roosevelt helped create some of the country's earliest national parks and forests. He signed laws protecting wilderness areas throughout the country.

Roosevelt helped to protect bison, an animal he had first seen out west.

A Great President

Teddy Roosevelt was a popular president. In 1904 he won election to another four years in office. Today many people think of him as one of our country's greatest presidents.

Glossary

canal a waterway that people dig across land to connect bodies of water

conservation the protection of nature and natural resources

strike an action by workers, in which they stop working as a way to get better pay or working conditions

wilderness wild land where people do not live